Devon
Haunted
Houses

Picture Credits
Cover image: © Shutterstock
Tree image: © Shutterstock
All other photographs: © Margaret Caine 2015

Designed by Alix Wood: www.alixwood.co.uk

Published by Orchard Publications
Orchard is an imprint of Tor Mark,
United Downs Ind Est, Redruth,
Cornwall TR16 5HY

First Published 2015

Text © Margaret Caine & Alan Gorton 2015

ISBN 978 1898964 94 7

Printed by Hedgerow Print, Marsh Lane,
Lords Meadow, Crediton EX17 1ES

Chambercombe Manor, Ilfracombe - EX34 9RJ

Wednesday, July 12, 1738, was a hot, dry day. Just the sort for Jan Vye to repair a hole in the roof of Chambercombe Manor. Standing at the front of the building, looking up, he was thinking about the materials he would need from his workshop. Now, for the first time he noticed the outline of what had been a window. Jan looked and looked. In his mind he compared the outside with the inside. He just couldn't match the outline of that window to any existing room inside. There were only four rooms on that floor but here were five windows. His father and mother had lived here for many years after buying the estate from Humphrey and Edward Harpur for £840, but had never mentioned anything about an additional room. Jan himself had lived with them before inheriting the estate when his father died in 1734, and he had never noticed the outline before.

Jan knew the house was old and he was aware of some of its chequered history. The estate had been mentioned in the Domesday Book of 1086 and there was a house here in 1162 which belonged to Sir Henry de Champernowne, Lord of the Manor of Ilfracombe. For the next four centuries de Champernowne's descendants lived in what was obviously a substantial and significant property before it passed to Henry Grey, Duke of Suffolk, whose daughter the ill-fated Lady Jane Grey visited on one occasion in the 1550s when she was a teenager. Then she was known for her beauty and her ability to write and speak Greek, Latin, French, Hebrew and Italian but this was before she was hurled into national politics. Most of the present building was put up by the Greys as a comfortable lodging when they visited their Devon estates. But for some reason the estate declined and the house itself became just a farmhouse. It didn't though lose its former grandeur. Long after even Jan had left, it was just waiting to be re-discovered and in 1979 was donated to the Chambercombe Manor Trust, who have restored its fabric and grounds. Now we can soak up its atmosphere – and keep a sharp eye for its ghostly inhabitants. For they are here, waiting for you.

But that day, Jan was puzzled: was a room hidden next to what is now 'Lady Jane's Room'? He spoke to his wife, who was as intrigued and together they went upstairs to where the 'hidden' room might be. Jan knocked on the wall – a hollow sound confirmed there was an empty space behind. He broke a small hole in the wall and poked a candle through – in the close, musty gloom they could just make out a four-poster bed surrounded by the tatters of rotting curtains. Here was a room which had been bricked up for many, many years! Later that day, they enlarged the hole and scrambled through, pulled the curtain aside and staggered back - for there, in the flickering, silent semi-darkness, on the dusty, decaying bedspread lay a gleaming white skeleton, fully clothed in a fine dress. On this hot summer's day the coldest chill ran up their spines.

Jan Vye rushed into town to tell the authorities what they had found. A local doctor examined the skeleton and reported that it was that of a young woman, though he had no way of identifying her or what had caused her death. But tongues wagged and soon it was accepted without any foundation, that the woman had died sometime during the six years between 1695-1701 when the house was tenanted by William Oatway. This may have been embroidered by the similarly unsubstantiated but accepted 'fact' that William's father, Alexander, a respected, influential citizen who fell on hard times, had become leader of a gang of notorious wreckers. On stormy nights it was said they lured ships seeking safe haven in Ilfracombe harbour onto the treacherous rocks, robbing and murdering any unfortunate crew or passengers who survived, plundering their possessions and cargo. William though was not one of them.

His mother had died when he was only three years old and he was often neglected in his childhood, but he had grown into a socially responsible, law abiding, man who – so the story continues – actually saved a beautiful Spanish woman from his father's wrecking ventures, then fell in love with and married her. In fact we know he married Ellen Gregory, whom he met when living with his uncle and aunt at Wallredon Lodge in Cornwall, where he had been sent to learn how to operate their tin mine. By an amazing coincidence though, William had actually been instrumental in rescuing Miss Gregory when she was travelling in a ship which was wrecked in Hele Bay – but not by his father's doings. Certainly William took out a lease on Chambercombe Manor which his father had neglected and gambled away. He and his wife were happy enough here but William was always sadly aware that as a tenant he would never be able to save enough money to buy the Manor outright and provide a family home that could be passed on to his descendants. They were nonetheless delighted when they had a baby daughter, whom they christened Kate.

When only 16 years old, Kate met and fell in love with an Irishman, Duncan Wallis, captain of a family-owned ship. The pair married and decided to live in Dublin. William Oatway and his wife were heartbroken but Kate promised to visit them as soon and as often as she could. With Kate gone, the house seemed empty and by implication so were William and his wife's lives. They knew they had to get used to Kate being away, but looked forward to seeing her again at some time.

This was a time of ferocious storms along the north Devon coast. As each tide ebbed, William would struggle onto the beach of Hele Bay as far as he could in the boiling surf to look for any ships in distress and offer whatever help he could to their stricken crew. He witnessed the horrors of the sea: bloated bodies floating around smashed rigging, mutilated beyond recognition by the rocks, some missing limbs or even heads, clothes torn from their bodies. On one of those early mornings, after a particularly bad night, as brooding thunderclouds indicated another approaching storm, bracing himself against the ferocious, howling wind and lashing rain, enduring the maelstrom of froth created by huge breakers, he heard a faint sound. It was no more than a low murmur. It came from rocks nearby. Compulsively, already affected by the carnage and destruction around him, he slipped and slithered over. The sound was coming from a badly injured young woman, barely alive, her body terribly gashed from the pounding onto the rocks, swollen, black and blue, her battered, bloodied face so pulverised it wasn't possible to distinguish her features. As carefully as he could, he carried her to his home at Chambercombe Manor where his wife tried desperately to save her life. But the woman's injuries were too grave. Later that night she died, without regaining consciousness.

Who was she, and how could they let her family know what had happened to her? Was there a clue in her large pearl necklace and many precious rings? Gently and tenderly and respectfully, William and his wife looked through her clothes for some clue to her identity. There was nothing to help, though they did find a money belt strapped around her waist containing enough gold, jewellery and coins to fund his one cherished ambition: to pay off his father's debts and buy Chambercombe Manor outright. Even for William, temptation was too strong. His hands shaking, he unfastened the belt from the dead body. That night, he slept fitfully, racked by guilt at what he had done.

After the storm had abated, a shipping agent called, enquiring if anyone knew anything about a female passenger missing off a wrecked ship. What a dilemma: if William admitted finding a young woman he would be accused of stealing her valuables and forced to return them. So he kept quiet. As he was leaving, the agent asked William to keep an eye on the coastline and contact him should the body of a young woman be washed ashore. She was Mrs Katherine Wallis.

What they had done struck William and his wife. Their beloved daughter had kept her promise, was coming home to see them, they watched her die and they had robbed her dead body. Grief stricken, William dutifully laid her in a room which was rarely used, and walled it up. Then he and his wife left Chambercombe Manor. They never returned. The pain was too much.

After Jan Vye and his wife found the skeleton, Kate Wallis's remains were buried in Ilfracombe parish church, next to her mother. But … though this explains the mystery of the hidden room found in 1738, Kate Wallis's ghost still walks along the corridors, to the chapel and to the cobbled courtyard, and a low moaning emanates from the secret room where her remains were found.

Kate Wallis is not though the only ghost here. Many visitors have seen and heard two small girls in upstairs rooms. Then there is a lady in a long white dress who walks near the pond. She is married but reaches out to a gardener standing nearby: while obviously lovers, the pair never actually touch. Recently mediums have identified several other spirits, a six-year-old girl in the 'Chippendale Room' and a friendly man in the 'Tudor Room'. Then on a particular day each September a crown in this 'Tudor Room' moves onto a Jacobean chest and a candle is put on the floor – by unseen hands. As recently as September 26, 2006, the TV programme *Most Haunted* filmed a child's crib rocking backwards and forwards without any human assistance.

Shelley's Cottage,
Lynmouth - EX35 6EF

On December 11, 1816, *The Times* reported that the lifeless body of a young woman had been pulled out of the Serpentine in Hyde Park. No-one knew who she was but she had an expensive ring on her finger and was in an advanced state of pregnancy. It was only later that she was identified as Harriet Shelley, the 21-year-old wife of the famous poet Percy Bysshe Shelley, from whom she was now estranged. Harriet Westbrook had met Shelley's younger sister, Helen, at school in Clapham, and through her the poet. She was then 15 and shortly after her 16th birthday in 1812 the couple eloped to Scotland; Shelley was 19. After a hasty marriage, they spent their honeymoon in Dublin and Wales before arriving in Lynmouth from Nantgwllt *via* Chepstow.

Initially, they were heading for Ilfracombe but were so attracted to Lynmouth that they decided to stay. Here they spent an idyllic summer at what was then called Woodbine Cottage, at the bottom of a cliff with Lynton perched above, and owned by a Mrs Hooper. Now listed Grade II, the two-storey building dates back to at least 1721 and is partly stone, partly plastered and limewashed rendered cob or rubble, with a thatch roof, ancient chimneys and two dormers. In 1952, a devastating flood caused such substantial damage that it was thought the cottage may have to be demolished. Fortunately, this wasn't so but after a succession of owners it fell into disrepair until in the 1990s it was completely restored.

The cottage was not entirely to Shelley's liking. In a letter dated July 5, 1812, to his friend William Godwin, he described how *"...we now reside in a small Cottage but the poverty & humbleness of the apartments is compensated by their number..."*. For some time, Shelley had wanted to establish an egalitarian and literary commune. He wasn't the sort of person to restrict his life-style to his limited finances but he knew his circumstances would improve in just one year when he was 21. But the relationship between Harriet and Percy Shelley was already under strain. They argued, mainly because Harriet's older sister, Eliza, had accompanied them on honeymoon and Shelley was paying her too much attention. With them, too, was their Irish servant, Dan Healy. Additionally, Shelley wanted to bring Elizabeth Hitchener, a like-minded schoolmistress at Hurstpierpoint who was 10 years his senior, William Godwin, the liberal thinker, Godwin's second wife Mary and their miscellany of children – with the Shelleys making a total of 13 people.

These were also turbulent times on the national scene. In the Spring of 1812 Prime Minister Spencer Percival had been assassinated. Workers were being urged to seek political power. The Government was anticipating riots. Here was work for Shelley's pen and Lynmouth offered the right atmosphere, undisturbed peace and the joys of the coast. He composed an early radical poem 'Queen Mab – A Philosophical Poem'. He also wrote a seditious paper, 'Declaration of Rights' and was seen wading into the bay to launch copies in sealed bottles and releasing boxes tied to balloons from the foreshore. The Town Clerk of Barnstaple reported this to the Home Secretary, Lord

Sidmouth. Shelley sent Dan Healy to Barnstaple to post copies but he was promptly arrested, and fined £200 or 6 months in the 'common gaol' in lieu of payment.

Shelley found being under observation irksome. With money he borrowed from his landlady, Mrs Hooper, he bribed a boatman to take him and his young bride across the Bristol Channel to Wales. From there, in the winter, they returned to London.

In London, Harriet's and Shelley's friendship turned sour. Nonetheless, on March 24, 1814, they went through a second marriage ceremony, this time at St George's, Hanover Square, because someone had raised doubts about the legitimacy of their earlier one. They already had a daughter, Eliza Ianthe, but Percy spent increasing periods of time away from home with Godwin and others. Within four months, Harriet had moved to Bath. They never lived together again.

As with Harriet, Shelley found Godwin's 16-year-old daughter, Mary, irresistible. The couple ran off to Europe – leaving Harriet pregnant with Shelley's second child. When Shelley and Mary returned, she too was pregnant. Some years later Mary Godwin became Mary Shelley who found fame as the author of 'Frankenstein'. Shelley though gave Harriet a large sum of money when she went to live with her father.

Over time, Harriet took several lovers and by 1816 was again pregnant. Her father refused to have her under his roof and in shame she took lodgings under the name of Harriet Smith. As her pregnancy progressed, Harriet became desperately unhappy and on November 9 she disappeared. She had written letters to her father, sister and husband, the latter ending *"... may you enjoy that happiness which you have deprived me of."*

During their time together at Lynmouth, Harriet had been truly happy – the only time in her short and tragic life. To this day, she walks about in Shelley's Cottage trying to recapture the special flavour of those days.

Tetcott - EX22 6QZ

There are magical overtones in the very words Arscott of Tetcott. The Arscotts were one of the ancient families of Devon freeholders who rose to the ranks of the squirearchy over a period of 300 years or so by the steady accumulation of land, mostly though marriage. In 1552, John Arscott purchased the Tetcott estate from the Earl of Huntingdon and started to build his new manor house. It was completed by his son. In extended form this is the one we see today.

A plaque above the doorway shows the date '1603' but don't be deceived as this came from the estate's corn mill which was built then. For over two hundred years the house remained home to five generations of Arscotts, all christened John. Some time during the reign of Queen Anne they built an imposing brick mansion to the side. We can get some idea of its size from the Hearth Tax records of 1647 when it had a total of fifteen hearths, putting it on a par with the largest houses in the county. However when the last of the John Arscotts died and the estate passed to a distant cousin, Sir William Molesworth of Pencarrow in Cornwall, it was dismantled. Now what we see is really a cluster of old houses, part built in the reign of Henry VII, part during the time of James I, and some under Queen Anne: all reflected the increasing wealth and significance of the family.

When the last John Arscott died in 1788, he had already become well known throughout the district for his eccentricities. He was not, though, the first of the family to become notorious. An earlier John – always referred to as the 'Wicked' Arscott for his habit of setting his big dogs on poor people and beggars as they approached his door – was lynched on an oak tree in the park. Many people have seen this re-enacted, in ghostly form.

This last John was a complex character. Outwardly, he was indistinguishable from any other country squire of the period, with long wig, long coat with silver buttons, breeches and high boots, and usually accompanied by a brace of greyhounds and a pointer. He was a fervent 'follower of the chase' hunting stag, fox and anything that ran, and he loved cock-fighting. As local squire, he was also responsible for settling disputes within the parish – though he got through these as peremptorily as possible so he could retire to the ale-house and get drunk. He was rather coarse, too, enjoying singing obscene songs and telling ribald stories.

He also lived in an almost medieval way complete with a dwarf jester, whom he named Black John. This latter's favourite party trick was to swallow a number of live mice with string tied to their tails and then pull them out from his stomach. Another was to 'mumble' a sparrow, gripping it in his teeth by its legs and then with just his lips stripping off its feathers until it was naked. Black John lived in a wooden hut close to the kennels, and when the dogs were hunting he ran with them, often being at the kill.

It is not easy to reconcile John Arscott's passion for hunting with his gentleness towards 'Old Dawty', his enormous pet toad which responded when he whistled or called it, leaping into his hand or onto his knee, and feeding at his table: not surprisingly, locals believed it to be his familiar. However, it proved mortal enough when another of his unusual pets, a raven, ate it. It was not only at home though that John Arscott behaved eccentrically: he was equally outrageous when he attended church. To while away what he regarded as the tedium of the services, he took jars full of flies to feed to the spiders, or pocketfuls of apples to throw at the parson, or he would call out if he thought the clergyman was reading the Bible badly. Perhaps this accounts for the tone of his epitaph in the parish church:

"Sacred to the memory of John Arscott of Tetcott in the Parish, Esq., who died the 14th day of January 1788. What his character was need not be recorded. The deep impression his benevolence and humanity has left in the minds of his friends and dependants will be transmitted by tradition to late posterity."

When the old squire died, Black John was inconsolable. He refused to leave the graveside and made a shelter near the churchyard wall, where he sobbed away what was left of his life, dying himself within a very short time.

As far as one can discover, John never married. He lived with one of his father's servants, Thomasine Spry, but never 'made an honest woman' of her, and died childless. Thomasine was buried at Tetcott in 1796, aged 76.

It is hardly surprising that this lively old boy haunts the district. You can see him in full gallop on his favourite horse, Black-Bird, blowing his hunting horn – as one would expect, in defiance of the hunting ban. If you don't actually see him, you will certainly hear him. And hunting he is.

Oldstone,
Blackawton - TQ9 7DG

Though completely destroyed by fire on Saturday, February 16, 1895, the ruins of Oldstone still reflect the age of grandeur and privilege it belonged to. It also has a mystery.

In Saxon times, Oldstone was owned by a local chieftain named Ulf. It was then given by William le Spek to the Canons of Torre, Torquay, who built a court house, now part of Oldstone Farm. For over 200 years, it belonged to the Cholwich family, powerful, wealthy merchants whose dynastic aspirations ended when the last male heir was imprisoned for debt. Fortunately, that was after they had largely rebuilt their Georgian style house in 1725. In the grounds you can see a bridge over the drive, a shell-lined grotto and a hermit's cave from when it was fashionable for every smart country property to have one at the bottom of the garden. It also has a ghost, a Victorian one, of a young lady. The tragedy leading to it has remained a mystery from the time of a famous trial in 1884.

Then the estate belonged to William Dimes, a barrister, and his wife, Martha. There, in December, 1861, their fourth and last child was born. She was named Laura Constantia. As she grew up, Laura thought Oldstone was a gloomy place. She was a single-minded, spirited girl, always challenging the accepted conventions of her time and the conservative outlook of her parents. They were not socialites and she had few opportunities to meet people of her own age – especially eligible young men. She was particularly unhappy after both her sisters married and left, Ellen in 1877 and Matilda in 1881, leaving Laura alone with her ageing parents and their staff. On the positive side she was an excellent horsewoman and was able to spend much of her time riding round the family park and surrounding area.

On Monday, 28 April, 1884, Laura went for an early morning ride and then took her collie dog, Juno, for a walk. Both were quite ordinary, normal things for her to do. She had changed into a blue day dress and straw hat though for some reason she continued to wear her riding gloves. An hour or so later her collie returned home. It was soaking wet though no one was surprised as Laura often played with it around the pools in the garden. But Laura didn't come home. Her parents organised a search – she had vanished.

The following day, Elizabeth Luckcraft, wife of one of the estate workers, was walking her own dog in the woods. Glancing across 'Monk's Pool', the higher and deepest of three in the mansion's grounds, she saw the top of a woman's straw hat, about three feet from the bank. Mrs Luckcraft bent down for a closer look – and recoiled in horror. Laura was standing bolt upright on the bottom of the pond, one arm stretched out in front, the water just covering the top of her straw hat. Mrs Luckcraft rushed back to the big house and told Laura's parents. They were devastated.

An inquest was held. The post-mortem examination revealed no sign of violence except for a small bruise on Laura's temple. There were no clear indications of drowning. Her clothing had not been disturbed.

There was no evidence she had struggled with any attacker. The coroner couldn't decide how she came to be in the water. A verdict of 'accidental death' was recorded. On Saturday, 3 May, after a service at St Saviour's, Dartmouth, Laura's body was interred at Longcross Cemetery, Townstal. And there the tragic affair might have ended. Every-one at Oldstone, grief-stricken parents and sorrowful servants, found the days and nights extremely difficult. They came to a climax less than three weeks later.

That was when it was discovered Laura had secretly married Hugh Shorland. He worked in a solicitor's office in Modbury but was not popular in the area and was regarded as disreputable. For some time he had spoken of his plans to emigrate to New Zealand where his father, allegedly a doctor, lived. But despite her parents' open disapproval as Shorland was five years older than her and had been involved in several dubious money-making schemes, Laura was determined to become his wife – in secret if need be. On Tuesday, 8 April, 1884, without telling anyone at home, she had ridden to Kingsbridge and the couple were married by special licence. Laura didn't start off on any adventurous honeymoon. After the wedding, she simply returned home. Two days later Hugh Shorland resigned from his job, saying he was going to New Zealand on a 'business' trip. He then wrote a letter to his new wife, which he asked a friend who was travelling to Brindisi to post from there. Presumably this was to keep up his pretence to Laura. Yet on the very day of Laura's death a postman saw Shorland in the neighbourhood. On the Wednesday following Laura's funeral, Shorland was discovered hiding in a cottage in Modbury. Admitting that he had never left the area, and indeed had been at this cottage all the time, he was arrested on suspicion of murder. But despite considerable circumstantial evidence – and gossip – there was not a shred of conclusive proof to convict him. The trial collapsed.

So what happened? Had Laura been murdered? Had she met Shorland in the woods? Had they argued? Did he push her into the pool and her feet became trapped in the soft mud and debris at the bottom? Had she committed suicide? Or was it all a tragic accident? The police closed the case. Perhaps they should have pursued the matter for other information, though again circumstantial, reached them not long afterwards. That summer, Shorland did leave for New Zealand - and trouble. In 1891 he was sentenced to two years imprisonment for libelling a young, unmarried woman. The evidence against him included a threat that he would force her to commit suicide, just as he had done to his wife in England! That doesn't of course amount to a confession, but does it account for Laura's ghost being so active?

That began in 1892 when the children of Laura's brother, William, who were visiting Oldstone mischievously locked the door of a room in which a chimney sweep was working. Before long he could be heard screaming, terrified, banging to get out. What had he seen? Only three years later, and ten years after Shorland's trial, a chimney set on fire. Within two hours the entire building was totally gutted. Strangely, the glass remained intact in the window of just one room - that called the 'Ghost Room' by those children. And it stayed there for many years. Ever since, a ghost of a woman has been seen leaning out of one of the mansion's ruined windows, bathed in light – from the devastating fire, we wonder? Then again, Laura's ghost has been seen frequently both by her graveside and in the grounds of Oldstone, around the ponds where she loved to walk with her dog. Also, a man in white and a woman in black have been seen standing very near the ruined mansion, possibly a bride and groom.

Laura Dimes is not the only supernatural appearance around here. When visitors to Longcross Cemetery are sitting on a bench, a man in nineteenth-century clothing appears, points out Laura's grave and emphasises that 'he' has got away with murder. Is this one of Laura's relatives or close friends seeking re-examination of the events surrounding her death or looking for retribution? Or could it be her husband, Hugh Shorland? If he was innocent, then perhaps he holds this lonely vigil at his wife's graveside, still seeking justice for her?

Laura is the only one who knows for sure what really happened that Spring day.

Devon is not very well provided with castles. One of the few is Berry Pomeroy, now a crumbling, romantic ruin which has not been inhabited for more than a century. It is really a Tudor mansion within the walls of an earlier castle built in the 14th century by the Pomeroy family on a precipitous crag above Gatcombe Brook. Even before they were recorded in the Domesday Book of 1086 the Pomeroys had held the land a long time. But by 1547, Sir Thomas Pomeroy was in financial difficulties and sold the estate to Edward Seymour, 1st Duke of Somerset. Apart from a short period of six years when it was forfeit to the Crown following Edward's beheading for treason in 1552, the castle has remained in his family. It was though abandoned in the late 17th century when the 4th baronet moved to Wiltshire because as Speaker of the House of Commons he felt he needed to be nearer to London. By 1701, the castle was a ruin and stayed that way for a hundred years until the end of the 18th century saw it celebrated as an example of the 'picturesque' aesthetic and become a popular tourist attraction – aided by its reputation of being the home of a large number of gloomy ghosts. The current count is a total of 26. You mustn't dismiss them lightly.

Primarily, Berry Pomeroy seems to be infested with evil. An air of melancholy lays over the whole place. Many visitors become cold and shivery as soon as they arrive, affected by an irrational, oppressive fear of something inexplicably repellent so overwhelming that they leave – and never return. Even after they have stayed and looked round, other people have felt the presence of spirits who wished them to be gone, and as twilight closes still others have seen faces peering at them from upstairs windows in the top storey at the back of the castle – though there are no floors left intact.

One ghost which is frequently seen is the White Lady. She is the sad spirit of Lady Margaret Pomeroy who lived here in the Middle Ages and who had the misfortune to fall in love with the same man as her sister, Lady Eleanor. Insanely jealous, Eleanor had Margaret imprisoned in the deepest dungeon. Here Margaret lived out of sight for 19 years until eventually she was left to starve to death. The crumbling masonry above that cell is still known as St Margaret's Tower, and she now haunts that area. She always appears dressed from head to foot in white – hence her name – her hair streaming wildly behind her.

The wicked Lady Eleanor's vengeful spirit also comes from the Tower. Legend says that to see her is to die, an omen that never fails – but actually it doesn't work, as many who have are very much alive.

Then there is the phantom of the Blue Lady. She was raped by her own father, a former lord of Berry Pomeroy. Subsequently, in one of the bedrooms she strangled the child which resulted from this incest. At the end of the 18th century her ghost actually appeared to Dr Sir Walter Farquhar, later Physician to King George IV, who at the time was practising in Torquay, and we can expect to be a reliable witness.

When he was attending the steward's wife who had lived at Berry Pomeroy for 30 years and had never seen the ghost, the doctor saw the apparition and later wrote:

If ever human face exhibited agony and remorse; if ever eye, that index of the soul, portrayed anguish uncheered by hope, and suffering without interval; if ever features betrayed that within the wearer's bosom there dwelt a hell, those features and that being were then present to me.

Other people describe how the Blue Lady rings her hands in anguish, with a look just as Dr Farquhar described. The murdered child has also been heard crying and screaming in the building.

Blue is also the colour of another ghost you must be careful of. This young but clearly malicious girl wears a quaint blue costume or is bathed in a blue light. She beckons to visitors, especially men, from the top and most perilous parts of one of the walls. Many people think she is frightened to move in case she falls and some have tried to climb up to rescue her but have themselves almost been killed by falling masonry when they are near the top. Others are sure she has tried to push unwary sightseers off the ramparts from where they can fall to certain death on the rocks below. Who is she? Is she a long dead member of the de Pomeroy family? Is she Isabella, the illegitimate child of a Baron de Pomeroy, who was murdered when she was just 9 years old? We have no evidence to her identity. But she's fiendishly active.

On March 14, 2005, a newspaper published a dramatic account of a medium spending a night at Berry Pomeroy. When she had parked her car in front of the Gatehouse she became too scared to get out. It was constantly rocked to and fro and she spent the night terrified, during which she saw The White Lady pacing up and down the Rampart Wall. TV investigators from the programme Most Haunted have also experienced considerable paranormal activity in the ruins and grounds. You have to be careful here!

Castel-a-Mare,
Torquay - TQ1 1RN

With its warm southerly, sloping aspect, in Victorian times Warberry Hill became a fashionable area of Torquay. From 1843, Jacob and William Harvey built a number of Italianate style properties aimed at attracting the wealthy, leisured folk who were 'taking the air'. The names of these new houses – Villa Maggiore, Sorrento, Capo-di-Monte - reflected the interests of their new inhabitants. Though many have since been turned into apartments, or demolished, the district still retains much of its former character and has been designated a Conservation Area. On September 29, 1852, a lease was granted to William Reed to build a property in Middle Warberry Road. From the beginning it was called Castel-a-Mare, and a map of 1866 uses this romantic name. However, by the early twentieth century the house had stood empty and neglected for some time, ever since, according to locals, a horrific double murder there – and it was haunted! They could hear sounds of laughter, of feet racing along corridors, and an intermittent blood-curdling scream. Few people wanted to live there.

One family who did rent it reported how, after various disturbing experiences, they made sure all the doors were locked before they went to bed and purposefully arranged twigs and leaves by the front door. Next morning, every single door was unlocked and wide open – but the twigs were intact! That very night, they heard the click of a latch and watched whilst the knob of the door began to turn – then opened just wide enough to let some-one through. But nothing visible appeared. Next they heard the sound of footsteps hurrying along the corridor above them, but again no one was there. They were also disturbed by a periodic piercing, unnerving scream by some-one in abject terror, which came from both inside the house and from the garden. Their visitors heard it, too. The tenants couldn't use the drawing room as it seemed full of unseen people moving about, and they frequently saw a strange woman in black on the staircase. Not surprisingly, they left – fled, actually.

Interestingly, there are three accounts of investigations of supernatural events here. The first was by Violet Tweedale, a spiritualist and medium who had written a good deal about the paranormal and lived in the same road, so was well acquainted with both the property and the stories. From about 1912, she and her husband held vigils in the house, describing them in her book Ghosts I Have Seen. She recorded a number of strange incidents, exactly as those described by the young tenants. A more dramatic visit was in 1917. During a séance, a small, frail medium became possessed by the spirit of an infuriated man who in a harsh, threatening voice and with violent language menacingly demanded to know what right they had to intrude on his privacy. At this point, the medium displayed superhuman strength and bellowed like a bull. Though now exhausted she was taken over by a different control, this time a woman, who wept broken-heartedly, pointing to one side of the room where her master had been strangled. Then she gave a piercing scream, just as visitors and locals had heard.

Some time later, again two entities took hold of the medium, one being a maid who years ago had witnessed a murder in the house and who herself was subsequently murdered – the double murder of the stories.

In 1926, the author Beverley Nichols wrote in his autobiography *Twenty Five* how in June one year during the First World War (about the same time as Violet Tweedale) he, his brother Paul and a friend, Lord Peter Saint Andries had visited Castel-a-Mare. They had heard stories of it being haunted, and not just the house but also the stables where frightened horses had to be forced in backwards, of how dogs out for walks howled as they passed, how no tenants would stay, and why eventually the house was left to deteriorate. They decided to explore.

At the back of the house, the three 'ghost-hunters' climbed through a basement window. With only a candle as light, and in Paul's case a crucifix to protect them, they went from room to room, eventually climbing up a narrow staircase to the top floor. Nichols then realised that his thought processes and body had begun to 'slow down' and he had become confused, "*as if an anaesthetic was beginning to take effect*". Then he fainted. The others carried him outside but Peter Saint Andries returned in alone, promising to whistle every minute to let the others know he was safe. For twenty minutes he searched the house and whistled, but then Nichols and his brother heard a terrifying shout from Saint Andries, with crashing and banging as if two people were in a frantic, violent struggle. Within minutes, a dishevelled Peter rushed out in a state of terror, covered in plaster and dirt, before he collapsed in the garden. When he recovered he described how, near the room where Nichols had fainted, he had seen a greyish light in the darkness and when he turned to go up the stairs something "*black, silent and man-shaped rushed from the room and knocked him to the floor … An overwhelming sense of evil overcame him and he struggled to keep his sanity as he ran from the house.*"

There are further reports about Castel-a-Mare. In the *Torquay Times* of 6 July 1962, a Miss Singleton of Bristol recalled how she and another medium had visited the property some years previously. As they were going up the stairs they had met a woman in black who appeared from nowhere and rushed past them, before Miss Singleton was pinned against the wall by a very strong force. On an earlier occasion, a visitor found himself confronted by a black mass, shaped like a man but without a face, which rushed at him and knocked him flat on his back, then attacked like three 'somethings'. Only then were the visitor and his friends told that Castel-a-Mare had been the scene of a brutal double murder in the latter part of the nineteenth century: that in a sudden and uncharacteristic moment of mental breakdown a doctor had strangled first his wife and then a maidservant who had seen the horrific incident taking place. Apparently, the small room where Nichols and Saint Andries had their experiences was where these crimes had been committed and from which the evil thing rushed at the visitor. The terrified screams which have been heard throughout the house are those of the maid.

Castel-a-Mare was demolished in 1920 and another built on the site. But the unusual phenomena continued. Since then, that house too has been knocked down and the site has been left empty – and still the blood-curdling noises continue!

So what had really happened at Castel-a-Mare? Were such sinister hauntings caused by equally sinister, dreadful crimes in peaceful Warberry? Certainly towards the end of the 19th century a doctor had lived in the house we can't find any record of a murder having been committed there. With the series of Jack the Ripper murders in London at the end of the 1880s, did the more imaginative neighbours cobble together a story based on some exaggerated report they had read? But if the story is correct and a gruesome double murder did take place, what happened to the bodies? Are they still waiting to be discovered underneath the green lawn? No search seems to have been instigated at the time. Had the doctor committed two perfect crimes and got away with them? We don't know but the paranormal activity continues.

Royal Castle Hotel, Dartmouth - TQ6 9PS

A utumn is the haunting season at the Royal Castle Hotel. And it is a royal ghost which haunts it. We are told she is Princess Mary (later Queen Mary II), wife of Prince William of Orange (William III). We can though be specific about the date and time: two o'clock in the morning on November 5 is when the ghostly sound of a horse-drawn carriage rattles and rumbles over old cobblestones which are no longer there. You never see it, nor when it clatters off again into the night: though at that time it's doubtful if too many of us will be awake.

The story goes that on Monday, 5 November 1688, 26-year-old Mary, daughter of King James II, was staying at this coaching inn. She was waiting anxiously for her husband who had planned to sail into Dartmouth with 400 ships and an army of 15,000 men to seize her father's throne. Mary was a poor sailor and had left the Netherlands ahead of the fleet (co-incidentally on the centenary of the Spanish Armada) to take advantage of calm weather before the winter winds set in. Dartmouth was regarded as a safe place for her as the South-West was generally opposed to James II and supportive of William and Mary's claim.

However, bad weather delayed William's fleet by a day and forced it to shelter in Torbay. He landed in Brixham harbour and immediately sent a messenger to ride with instructions for Mary to get ready for a carriage that would bring her to him. It seems that the lone horseman arrived in the dead of night: the clattering of hooves that marked his hasty entry into the inn are what we hear first, echoing through time. Just as in 1688, later you can hear the rumble of wheels crunching over cobbles as an invisible carriage rattles into the long-gone courtyard. Footsteps echo, doors open and slam shut, muffled voices speak, the princess and her ladies-in-waiting climb into the carriage with a squeaking sound like the springs on one side, the team of horses is whipped up and they then set off on their journey to reunite the royal couple and to the throne of England. The bell of St Saviour's church tolls two o'clock. The haunting ends – until next year.

So if the ghost is that of Mary, why should it commemorate a visit which presumably was a pleasant one? Why was an impression created strong enough to last more than 300 years? Is it connected with the date, as had not bad weather delayed the prince's landing their reunion would have coincided with his birthday (4 November), which was also the anniversary of their wedding day? Is it because Mary was here not knowing what had happened to her husband, not knowing if an uncertain military campaign lay ahead of her?

While the frisson of romance adds to this ghostly manifestation's appeal, the events are not historically correct. In the first place, Mary did not arrive in advance – she followed her husband William in Spring,

1689, when the throne was safely theirs. Secondly, roads around Dartmouth were so poor that although pack-horses could use them, a carriage most certainly could not. Finally, the Royal Castle Hotel simply did not exist: it was still two private houses owned by local merchants and was not converted into an inn until the following century.

So, assuming that the origin of these noises is supernatural, royal connection or not, what could be causing them? They may be connected to the mysterious death of William Tabb who worked in the stable at the rear of the hotel, but who one morning in 1895 was found drowned in the horse trough. The doors to the yard were still locked, so no-one really knows precisely what happened though at the time it was presumed he was the victim of a tragic accident. But the ghost of his body can be seen in the phantom trough, his legs dangling over the side. Nor is his the only hostler's ghost here. Darkie Chase lived over the stables and his ghost has been seen many times on its way downstairs.

These are not the only ghostly goings-on. Relatively recently, in 2004, near the staff room on the top floor, a woman wearing the normal housekeeping uniform – blue trousers and a white apron - held open the fire door at the back of the building. She appeared to be about 35 to 40 years old, with long, curly blonde hair reaching almost to her waist, smiled at other members of staff - then disappeared without a sound. Strangely, though, that fire door has a loud and distinct clatter as it closes.

Residents, too, have been involved. One in room 22 on the top floor in 1972 reported a lady wearing a flowing white dress walking along the balcony overlooking the central courtyard. In November 1979, the Gazette reported a visitor's intention to sleep in this haunted bedroom. She stayed awake until 2.30am, but as nothing unusual happened settled down to sleep. Then things really warmed up! Within moments she was shaken by an unseen hand. No one was there. From then she was kept awake by a thumping sound, which became so agitated her bed began to shake. At 5am her alarm clock, set for 7am, went off. She re-set it to get some sleep but it went off again: in all, it rang three times before 7am. She left the hotel convinced of the hauntings.

Mount Boone, Dartmouth - TQ6 9PB

In 1681 a black and white marble memorial in honour of Thomas Boone was put up in St Clement's church at Townstall on the edge of Dartmouth. About the same time, the same man was commemorated on a wooden board at St Petrox church, describing how he gave *"to ye Poare of this towne £10 pr Annvm to be for ever Payd by his heirs."* What is this all about?

Thomas Boone was born in 1610 in Townstall, became the local squire and in 1635 acquired land from which he began to build create the Mount Boone estate. Eventually, this stretched along the top of Ridge Hill on the north side of the town and across the River Dart to beyond Lipton. He soon built a substantial property reflecting his status as one of Dartmouth's more prominent men. By the start of the Civil War in 1642, it had become known as 'Mount Boone'.

Despite the Royalists taking Dartmouth in 1643, Thomas Boone was a staunch Parliamentarian and stepped in as its MP in 1646, just as it was won back from the Royalists. He continued as an MP until December 1648, earned the respect of his political colleagues and became a personal friend of Oliver Cromwell, serving him on diplomatic missions to Denmark, Sweden and Russia. In 1654 he was again elected as MP for Dartmouth and although he appears to have been highly regarded by the townsfolk the town's hierarchy, the 'Freemen' (an 'honour' they had bought) felt threatened by this 'incomer' and spent huge sums (the equivalent of £10,000 today) in legal fees to try to stop him becoming MP in 1658, arguing that only they should be electors, as was the tradition. Envy ruled. It was though the death of Oliver Cromwell which put an end to Boone's political career. He returned to Dartmouth and used the wealth he had built on the Newfoundland trade to extend and improve his house overlooking the town and the Mill Pool. After his death the property passed through several generations of the Boone family until it was sold to John Seale, an extremely rich merchant from London and the Channel Islands. His descendants enlarged and improved the house and estate until in 1879 Colonel J H Seale sold it. The house was demolished and in 1899 the estate was broken up into plots for auction. Parts of Mount Boone's high garden wall survive and in 1905 the Royal Naval College took over some of the estate lands while the area and the streets from the early road to the property have retained the original name – Mount Boone.

Many folk found Thomas Boone assertive, combative and abrasive but his daughter Anne was not in the least intimidated when he disapproved of the man she had fallen in love with. Unfortunately her suitor, Francis Drake, baronet of Buckland, was also the nephew of Sir Francis Drake whom Boone regarded as no more than a pirate: the family couldn't be trusted. Though father and daughter's relationship was decidedly strained, and she had inherited much of his character, eventually he forced her to make a solemn vow breaking off the engagement. Not long afterwards, on Monday, 26 January, 1679/1680, Thomas Boone died. Immediately the girl renounced her promise and before long the happy couple were settling into the comforts of Mount Boone.

However, in the grave as in life, Thomas Boone couldn't accept this. He had been used to getting his own way. His angry ghost began a campaign of harassment. It lit spectral lights, uttered unearthly noises and heaved heavy furniture about. As Anne walked around the house or garden, the ghost followed. The stress was intolerable, her health suffered and on medical advice she and her husband moved to London. Her father's ghost simply moved with them. They returned to Mount Boone, and the haunting continued.

Winter was approaching, the young wife's health was fragile and local clergymen were called on to exorcise Boone's ghost. After a tremendous spiritual struggle, Thomas Boone himself appeared in the room. Those present were terrified as he made an offer – he would leave the house on condition that his daughter accompanied him to the grave. The clergymen adjourned to the banks of the nearby stream at Castle Mill (we estimate by the Hermitage Castle, Old Mill Creek) to discuss this macabre suggestion. After a while, they accepted but first Thomas had to empty all the water from the stream using just a cockle shell – which they knew had a hole in it. Thomas agreed, though he did threaten his daughter that she would soon see just how he felt! Relieved that the ghost would be kept busy for ever, Anne and her husband went back to their house. Thirteen weeks later, she died. She had not enjoyed her peace for long – as her father had predicted.

Despite the charity recorded in the church, Thomas Boone's ghost is still ill at ease, and continues to haunt the site of his ancestral home. You can hear the clattering of his horse's hooves as he rides through the former courtyard, and he has been seen both on horseback and on foot.

In the area there is another modern ghost to look out for. It is that of an old woman who has been seen so often since she started on the Passenger Ferry between Kingswear and Dartmouth that she is known as the 'The Grey Granny' because she wears a grey coat. Even whole groups of people, the skipper, deckhands and travellers have seen her at the same time – but by the time the ferry gets to Dartmouth she has disappeared. As she's been seen on different ferry boats it's unlikely to be the boat that is haunted. So why is she here? To enjoy the trip?

Royal Naval College, Dartmouth - TQ6 OHJ

Most people associate Dartmouth with Britannia Royal Naval College. It opened on this site on September 14, 1905, though the town has been connected with the training of officer cadets since 1863 when the wooden warship HMS *Britannia* arrived to be the Officer Training College. Much more recently, a member of the Curator's staff at the College museum had an unnerving experience.

The morning started ordinarily enough, but the man did notice a young woman walking across the the Quarterdeck (the great hall on the ground floor of the College) from near the ladies' toilets and into classroom 04. This wasn't being used and thinking she may be lost he looked in to see if he could help – but there was no one there: the room was empty. Where was she? He was absolutely sure she had gone in there.

Now this is where it gets rather extraordinary. September 18, 1942, was a calm, sunny, cool day. Traditionally, the College's Christmas Term started that week but for once it had been postponed for seven days. This delay avoided a catastrophe. At 11.22am, in broad daylight, six airplanes swept out of low cloud at Noss Combe and flew low up the Dart. Few people took much notice, assuming they were 'our lads'. They weren't. They were German Fokke-Wulf 190 single-seat bombers. The planes dived over Dartmouth in a single concerted movement, two attacking the College, two the shipping and two the Noss shipyard. The raid had been carefully planned and was brilliantly executed by well-trained pilots. Dartmouth was unprepared even though on March 20, 1941, the Luftwaffe had begun to systematically destroy Plymouth, and on May 3, 1942, for more than an hour German aircraft dropped fire-bombs onto Exeter.

At Dartmouth, one bomb made a direct hit on the College's B block, causing extensive blast damage to its walls, roof and windows; the other hit the Quarterdeck. It was fortunate so few students were around. But there was one fatality, WRNS Petty Officer Mrs Ellen Victoria Whittall. Females had been enrolled only from April, 1940, and she was one of the first. Where the Curator's assistant had been when he saw the young woman was not far from where she died – as she was crossing the Quarterdeck she was actually walking from one bomb into the other, for one landed where the toilets are and the other where 04 is. According to records, Petty Officer Whittall had been in the toilets when the air raid took place – presumably intending to go into the classroom.

What the Curator's assistant saw is not the only phenomenon connected with Petty Officer Whittall's death. From time to time, all the lights on one side of the corridor come on, one after another at about half-second intervals, but nobody is ever at the light switches. When that happens people have been standing at exactly the spot where the young woman's ghost has been seen. The Curator's assistant is by no means the only one.

West Chapple Farm, Winkleigh - EX19 8PA

Tuesday, September 23, 1975, was an ordinary day in Winkleigh. It was warm, dry and most of the villagers were at work, the majority harvesting in the fields. A deliveryman had almost finished his rounds and as he went through the gate at West Chapple Farm he was whistling loudly so that the dogs would know he was there and wouldn't be startled. In fact, he was the one startled. As he got near to one of the barns he was confronted by a gruesome, horrifying sight:

two bodies were sprawled out on the ground and he could see just beyond the farm's front door a third one in the garden. Blood was splattered about each of their heads. Shaking, he turned round and rushed to the village police house to report what he had seen.

The Luxton family had been here for at least 600 years and could trace their ancestry back to Robert Luggesdon in the 14th century. The last individual owner was Robert John Luxton, a successful farmer who won prizes at fat stock shows and was a Church Warden at All Saints, Winkleigh. But he was also a straight-laced and tight-fisted man who denied any sort of normal life to his three children, Frances the eldest, Robert (known as Robbie) and Alan.. It was not that the elder Robert was stuck in a time warp. They had a wireless from about 1923, a car, and later an old tractor, but no electricity, no mains water. Some people regarded him as reclusive and a bit of an anachronism. It was Frances he was particularly hard on and she was never allowed to have boy-friends. He would deter any 'suitor' by riding behind Frances as she walked down the lanes with the boy. 'Romances' don't survive that sort of behaviour.

When Robert died in 1939 he left the farm in equal proportions to his three off-springs but without being more specific – a recipe for trouble. Nonetheless, the three siblings all lived here in some sort of harmony. They continued to run it as their father had done, now with Robbie in charge. At that time in the 1940s they ran it well. Their methods were similar to their neighbours but as tractors and combine harvesters became common they were left behind, still harvesting their crops in stooks, carrying their hay and straw home on a trailer. It was exceptionally hard work for the siblings, and they had only two labourers to help.

There were times when both Frances and Alan would willingly have left. They wanted their independence and to escape the gloomy world of West Chapple but Robbie always managed to prevent them, pleading that they had a responsibility to ensure it stayed in the family. Alan became a member of the Young Farmers' Club and learned from other sons and daughters about modern agricultural management and practices but again Robbie refused to agree to any changes. Although Alan had a third share he was paid a wage for his work just like the employees. It seemed that Robbie had inherited his father's suspicion, his almost paranoid fear of intrusion, his harsh morality and resistance to change, insisting they should farm as their predecessors had done with traditional methods adhered to strictly. After the end of the Second World War Alan had become engaged to a local girl but Robbie and Frances disapproved, fearing he would move away and they refused to let him have his third share in money. The engagement was broken off. Alan was never the same. He had a breakdown which required a spell in hospital. When he was allowed home it was noticeable just how much he had changed. He remained depressed and withdrawn, refused to change his clothes or leave his bedroom for long periods of time, and spent all his time alone.

Villagers noticed that as time went by they saw less and less of the three Luxtons, and some recalled that by 1975 Alan in particular had not been outside the farm for about twenty years. Frances too rarely ventured out unless she was going to attend the family graves at Brushford nearby, where occasionally she could be seen huddled over the tombstones in the dark churchyard.

By 1975, Frances was 67, Robbie 65 and Alan 60. They knew they couldn't carry on indefinitely. Even then it was becoming too much for them. All three were getting too old to run the farm as they had done, undertaking all the heavy work themselves, caring for the animals, managing the machinery and workshop and so on, even though to a limited extent they had moved with the times: they had brought in electricity, had a phone and mains water – but no such things as a television. Alan's health was also a problem. They quarrelled and the arguments turned to threats. Robbie became ill with worry, Frances depressed. All three had had enough. With regret, they decided to sell up. They accepted an offer of £90,000 for the farm and villagers thought they would buy a modern bungalow in Crediton and retire there. But having agreed a sale was easier than actually leaving. That was more than the Luxtons could bear. As the handover date approached Frances argued that they were born on the farm and should die there; Alan's mental state declined further and his distress was obvious to the other two. They always seemed to be arguing about what they should do. The arguments were settled on September 23, 1975. All three were found dead by the deliveryman.

An inquest was held. The pathologist reported that each of them had severe head injuries from a shotgun. One of the Luxton's labourers who had worked at the farm since 1953, Fred Lyne, gave evidence about the siblings' relationships (and quarrels). The Coroner declared that Alan had shot himself in the small hours of September 23; an hour or so later Robbie, finding Alan dead, had shot his sister Frances and then turned the gun on himself, committing suicide. What a tragedy. Forty years of claustrophobic rage, bred mostly in silence, had preceded the deaths.

The Luxton siblings had no direct heirs. The farm was sold lock, stock and barrel. The parishioners of All Saints church, Winkleigh, were grateful to receive a large legacy for restoration of their church where Robbie had worshipped for many years – the church and tower was re-roofed, organ overhauled, electric wiring renewed, oil-fired central heating installed. At Brushford where Frances had worshipped another legacy provided funds for restoration of that church, too. Frances was buried in the churchyard. Robbie and Alan were cremated at Barnstaple. A memorial service for all three was held in All Saints when at least 120 people attended. The siblings never knew they were so respected and had so many friends.

But the three Luxtons have never left the farm. Later owners have described noticing areas where they feel intense despair, bitterness and anger. Their ghosts have been seen at West Chapple and numerous folk have seen them in Winkleigh, while a ghost resembling Frances has also been seen sitting on the bench in Brushford churchyard.

Oldway Mansion, Paignton - TQ3 2TF

For the purposes of confidentiality, we have changed the real names of the three people recently involved in this story, but kept those from earlier times.

Young people from Torbay who wish to study the visual arts for A levels are particularly fortunate. Their sixth-form college offers a wide-ranging curriculum including the opportunity to specialise in photography, which encompasses not only the varying aspects of composition but the more technical developing, processing and printing of the exposed film. It is a popular course and two young ladies, Rosamund Catlin and Elizabeth Walford were among the most enthusiastic. They photographed their families, pets, friends and then graduated to searching out unusual features of the landscape and buildings and of course the sea, fishing boats, pleasure craft, children playing on the beach. All the time they were improving their techniques and then spent hours developing their films. They were fortunate too in that the college's Deputy Head was a constant source of inspiration, encouraging them to challenge themselves further.

Rosamund and Elizabeth were aware that Oldway Mansion housed the local Council Offices and had heard of its magnificent interior but had never been inside. It was the Deputy Head, Mrs James, who suggested that it might offer suitable subjects for the girls to photograph. They obtained permission and met the caretaker who would let them in when the offices were not occupied. Then one Saturday afternoon in late June, just before the end of their Summer Term, they walked up the drive with their bags of equipment. It wasn't a particularly pleasant day. It had rained earlier and was still overcast, but that enabled them to stop and take photographs of angles of shadows on bushes and unusual images of the exterior of Oldway.

It was in 1871 that Isaac Merritt Singer, founder of the Singer Sewing Machine Company, had bought the 17-acre Fernham estate. He had been born in Pitstown, New York, in 1811 and patented the Singer Sewing Machine in 1851. In the following twelve years he devised no fewer than twenty improvements. Now he wanted a new house. He immediately commissioned a local architect to build a new mansion, with instructions, "I want a big Wigmam and I shall name it 'The Wigwam'". The existing buildings were demolished and work begun. The Riding and Exercising Pavilion (a round building with a movable wooden floor for children's parties, of which he was particularly fond) was finished in 1873 but two years before the house was projected to be completed Isaac Singer died on July 23, 1875, aged just 63. The projected cost had been a staggering £200,000 and local folk couldn't imagine what it would look like. Isaac Singer left 22 living children and various ex-wives and mistresses but the third of his many sons, Paris Eugene Singer, took over. Paris did not like his father's choice. With even more grandiose ideas, he wanted a house to reflect his flamboyant life style. He decided on one modelled on the Palace of Versailles, with the eastern end inspired by the Place de la Concorde in Paris. Inside the 100-room mansion, a grand staircase would dominate the entrance, made of marble with bronze balusters, its ceiling ornately decorated with a design from Versailles, while a gallery on the first floor was a reproduction of the Hall of Mirrors there. It is hardly surprising he changed its name from The Wigwam to Oldway. To complete his project, Paris had the gardens laid out in Italianate style. It took until 1904 before it was ready.

While he was living at Oldway, Paris met and began an affair with Isadora Duncan, an equally eccentric personality, famous as an expressionist dancer. Whenever she was in England, she lived with Paris and together they had a son, Patrick. But their affair fizzled out, Paris Singer took American citizenship (partly because of the more favourable tax arrangements) and went to live there. Oldway ceased to be the permanent home of the Singer family. From then it had a chequered history. In the First World War it was used as an American Women's War Relief Hospital, then in 1929 became Torbay Country Club, when tennis courts and a bowling green were added. During the Second World War it accommodated RAF cadets training to be air crew and in 1943 was damaged in an air raid. In 1946, Paignton Urban District Council bought it from the Singer family for £46,000 for Council offices, though in 2013 plans were approved for the listed Grade II* property to be converted into a luxury hotel and retirement apartments: negotiations are still in progress.

Rosamund and Elizabeth knew only scraps of Oldway's history, and nothing of Paris Singer and Isadora Duncan. But that didn't matter as the caretaker let them in and they saw for the first time the woodwork's ornate features, the decoration, wall paintings and the marvellous staircase. The girls decided to start at the bottom and work their way to the top, taking photographs from varying angles and incorporating the different light, shadows and colours. They were absorbed for several hours until they finished along a corridor with bright wallpaper of flowing shapes and colours. After thanking the caretaker who had left them to get on with their project, they returned home, pleased with what they had achieved.

It was Monday before they could begin to develop their films in the college's dark room. This took them until well into the middle of the afternoon - and as they examined the last of their negatives they wondered what they had taken. They had photographed the unmistakeable figure of a woman in a flowing, ankle-length, loose fitting dress, a long scarf or shawl around her neck, her hair about her shoulders, her arms flung above her head, her body contorted in what seemed to be an exotic dance posture. And at the bottom corner of the negative were the letters 'I D'. Elizabeth and Rosamund recognised the corridor in Oldway but couldn't understand why a woman was there – they certainly hadn't seen her on Saturday and the caretaker had assured them that no-one was in the building. And why 'I D': where had that come from? They might have been disappointed by their work, but in fact the girls were terrified as here was something they had neither expected nor noticed and were sure didn't exist in reality.

So they rushed to their Deputy Head's room. Mrs James, was busy filling out reports but listened to the girls, pointing out the possibility of a rational explanation, some image on the wallpaper which after all was in flowing colours and abstract shapes, some trick of light, even some super-imposition from an earlier photograph. The girls couldn't accept any of these. They knew they had photographed something which did not exist. Their tutor didn't wish to dampen their previous enthusiasm and went with the girls to the darkroom, intending to point out the technical problem in their processing which had caused them to be so upset. She looked at the negative – and staggered back. She saw unmistakably just what the girls had described. Trying to hide her feelings, she suggested they print out the negative. They did – and the three of them stared at it. There was nothing on it except the empty corridor. Together, they all went to the library to research the history of Oldway and its occupants. What they found disturbed them further.

Isadora Duncan had indeed been famous – and infamous – world wide as a pioneering modern dancer but was just as notorious for her eccentric life-style. She had had two children, but never married. Both 13-year-old Deidre and 3-year-old Patrick died in an accident on the River Seine on April 19, 1913. They were in a car with their nanny, returning home after lunch with Isadora and Paris, when the driver swerved to avoid a collision with another car and the engine stalled. He got out to hand-crank the engine but had forgotten to set the parking brake. The car rolled across the Boulevard Bourdon, down the embankment and into the river. Both the children and the nanny were drowned. Isadora and Paris returned to Oldway, where a distraught Isadora tried to escape from her distress and grief by immersing herself in her dancing, performing alone and unnoticed, using the whole building as her stage.

Much later, Isadora's fondness for flowing dresses and scarves contributed to her own death in a car accident in Nice. She was wearing a hand-painted silk shawl, a gift from a friend, on the cold night of September 14, 1927, and refused to wear a cape as she settled into the rear seat of an open-topped Bugatti. The long shawl draped around her neck became entangled in the open-spoked wheels and rear axle, hurling her from the car and breaking her neck.

So what had the girls photographed? It could be nothing but Isadora Duncan's grief, so deep and consuming it has remained ever since at Oldway.

On Monday August 30, 2004, the *Mostly Haunted* Investigation Team received a photograph taken at a recent wedding in Oldway. It showed a clear 'anomaly' some sort of orb, a hazy, light grey colour with a bright lighter white patch between the bride and the photographer. Those who have seen it believe it to be the spirit of the bride's dead father – but was this, once more a sad Isadora Duncan – never the bride – dancing her way through eternity?

Exeter Prison - EX4 4EX

At 8am on Tuesday, April 6, 1943, 33-years-old Gordon Horace Trenoweth was hanged at Exeter prison. He was the last man to be executed there. Ever since, his ghost has haunted the place.

Three-and-a-half months earlier, on December 24, 1942, Trenoweth had murdered 61-year-old Albert Bateman who owned a small tobacconist shop in Commercial Chambers, Arwennack Street, Falmouth. Bateman was one of those people who never varied his habits. Though the period leading to Christmas was always a busy time, on Christmas Eve he didn't return home for the meal his wife had prepared. This was most unusual. Not surprisingly, she was worried. So she walked to the shop to find out why he was late. The doors were locked, no-one answered as she knocked and called out. She shouted louder and knocked frantically – but got no response.

She ran to the police station to report her fears. The police forced the door – and found Albert Bateman lying dead in a pool of blood on the floor. It was obvious to them that he had been beaten unmercifully. But there was also a revolver, a Webley, on the shop counter. They presumed this had been left by his murderer. There was no trouble tracing the revolver to Plymouth Docks and the police decided that it had been in the possession of Gordon Horace Trenoweth.

Trenoweth was already known to the police. His wife had been an in-patient at a mental hospital since 1941 and Trenoweth himself had recently completed a prison sentence for failing to pay for her care. When released, he had gone to live at his parents' house and it was there on Christmas Day that he was arrested.

There was a great deal of forensic evidence linking Trenoweth to Albert Bateman's shop. Fibres found on the revolver matched those of his jacket; an inside pocket had traces of gun oil; he was carrying two packets of cigarettes and a bank note which was positively identified as coming from the tobacconist shop as it had been torn and then repaired by a piece of paper carrying the shop's letterhead (a habit of Mr Bateman's); bloodstains on his clothes were the same type as the victim's. But at the trial there was a problem. Trenoweth denied any involvement with the murder and produced three witnesses confirming his alibi for the time of the murder, which was accepted at 6pm. The owner of a coal yard was sure that just before then Trenoweth had called asking if there was any work there, and Trenoweth's father and sister were equally sure that he had arrived home at 5.40pm and stayed there until at least 6.30pm. If these three were to be believed, Trenoweth could not have committed the crime. On the other hand, other witnesses described how Trenoweth had been spending money rather freely just after the murder. This, though circumstantial, allied to the forensic evidence, was sufficient. The jury returned a 'guilty' verdict but made a recommendation for mercy. The former was accepted, the latter was not. The judge put on the black cap and intoned the death penalty.

Some three decades later, two prisoners serving their time in the prison saw a man walking along a landing to a cell door – where he faded away and vanished! Frightened by this, they reported what they had seen but the prison officers staff paid little attention to their story. The men though were clearly upset and persisted to badger the staff. Only after several weeks did the Governor decide to investigate. Then it was discovered that the cell which the prisoners had described was the former condemned cell and, moreover, the description they gave of the mysterious disappearing man matched the physical description in prison records of Gordon Horace Trenoweth.

The condemned cell was bricked up and sealed but there are continuing reports of footsteps walking along this upper landing and of the shadowy figure of Trenoweth passing along. You could argue that this has become part of prison lore passed down from inmate to inmate but the sightings have been so frequent and by people who have not heard of the manifestations before that one has to give them credibility.

Totnes - TQ9 5SY

Founded early in the tenth century by the Saxon kingdom of Wessex as a fortified borough against the Danes, Totnes is now a small, genteel market town on the River Dart, known for its historic architecture, its location as a holiday centre between Torbay and Dartmoor and its recent evolution as a focus for all manner of 'New Age' lifestyles. It is not particularly famous for its ghosts yet it does have them, as you will discover if you are in the right place at the right time – so keep on the look-out!

With its origins lost in the past, no one knows exactly how old the Kingsbridge Inn in Leechwell Street is, but it is certainly the oldest in

45

the town. Parts of the building are fourteenth century, though most of what we see today is from the seventeenth. It is also one of the most haunted buildings in Totnes, the scene of strange happenings and unexplained apparitions. The most persistent is a woman, Mary Brown, who worked here as a barmaid during the seventeenth century. She was seduced and later murdered by her employer-landlord, who bricked up her body in the walls of the building. This story of ill-treatment by a man could well have an element of truth as she reveals herself only to women – many of whom take days to get over the experience. Mary was tall, with dark hair, and has been seen at the top of the stairs, startling anyone who comes face to face with her such as the young daughter of the family who kept the inn during the 1970s. The ghost was particularly active when the next owners were at the inn. A report in the *Morning Advertiser* of July 1, 1980, described how a tall, dark, quiet woman had often been seen by various people, standing at the bar or gliding through the kitchen where the staff had grown quite used to seeing her. The landlady was quoted, *"When I first came to the property I didn't know anything about a ghost but I felt freezing cold and at times even now I feel as though some-one is watching me. The first time I saw her was just after we moved in some 18 months ago. I looked through a window and saw a figure in the corner of the bar. It was a tall woman but she suddenly vanished."* The owner's dog was also aware of something and would bark at empty tables, as do the dogs which live at the inn today.

The inn changed hands again in October 1989 and both the new owners saw the woman, who always wore her hair in a bun. On at least one occasion, her reflection has been seen in a glass door – though that couldn't have been of anyone present as no-one had their hair in her style. At other times, she has also been seen sitting by the fire in the Pump Room but again no one has come through the door. A medium visiting the inn for the first time took a step back in alarm from the old pump in the Pump Room, and told the owners that there should always be a bright light shining there – advice they took. Have all these visitors and staff seen Mary Brown? Certainly, her appearances have continued unabated.

There is a house in South Street with an unusual name, Swansfoot. It also has an unusual story. By 1990, the property had become dilapidated and while working on the house builders found a small cavity in a partition on the front wall. Inside was the desiccated foot of a swan. The new owner could find no explanation for such a bizarre relic, but within a week he did begin to notice odd occurrences, and then distinctly heard a sound like the beating of wings and the noise of a large bird scrabbling about on the roof. He showed the foot to a number of people, and some remembered stories of a ghostly swan that flew up from the river at nightfall, circling slowly and landing, rather awkwardly, on the roof of the house. A poacher had once lived here but whether the appearance is related to the theft of one of the royal birds, or just its foot, no one knows. Or even if the other foot is still hidden in the house's walls!

The tall houses on Plymouth Road were built in the 1840s by Isambard Kingdom Brunel for the engineers and craftsmen constructing the ingenious but impractical Atmospheric Railway between Newton Abbot and Totnes. At that time the houses gave their residents uninterrupted views of the railway line's progress. One of them is haunted. The one which contained the drawing office was occupied by a man for over 40 years before he moved into an old folks' home, where he died. Now he returns. He wears ordinary clothes, is solid enough but never speaks. He goes into the bedrooms or bathroom, and is sometimes accompanied by a woman who brushes her hair, watched by the man. If you don't take any notice he moves objects around or makes noises to remind you he is here. Clearly, he wishes to retain his connection to the house.

'Grey Ladies' pop up in many places. They have been recorded since at least the 16th century, and may have started as folk memories of the nuns who cared for the sick throughout the Middle Ages. Not surprisingly they are frequently associated with hospitals. One (or more than one) has been seen in several parts of Totnes and Bridgetown – whether it is the same one walking about we can't be sure. She often appears at the ancient Leechwell, and may be associated with the wells which folk believed had healing properties for snake bite, skin disease and blindness, a belief descended from pre-Christian nature spirits. She has been seen in Maudlin Road, where the medieval leper hospital of St Mary Magdalen stood before it was demolished. Local legend suggests that patients went from here to bathe at the wells, so the Grey Lady may have accompanied them – but unfortunately there is no evidence that there were ever nuns here as the chapel was served by Benedictine monks from Totnes Priory. She has been seen quite frequently at Warland where there was another medieval chapel, dedicated to St Katherine, but again this was served by friars, not nuns, so if she did stay there she was being very naughty. Finally, a Grey Lady has been seen in a garden below the Cottage Hospital – appropriately so, but unfortunately it dates only from 1901.

Bowden House has so many ghosts it's difficult to dis-entangle them. Cats, dogs, monks, children, Elizabethans and Regency dandies have all appeared to visitors and staff. People have reached out and had their hand taken by unseen entities. Monks, presumably Black Canons, are quite frequent and you can hear them chanting in the main house and in the courtyard. One monk in a black habit with a knotted cord round his waist and his cowl emitting a blue light leans on visitors' beds for over ten minutes at a time. Another, in a brown habit, walks slowly about the nursery of the main house, and his cowl, too, emits a light so bright that the whole room is illuminated. In the library it isn't unusual to glimpse a figure through a crack in the door leading to what was a powder closet in the 18th century: when the door is opened, the figure vanishes. On August Bank Holiday 1988, people in several groups saw the ghost of a little girl with auburn hair, wearing a long blue dress, standing on the stairs and also sitting on a chair in the Pink Room. She was not a member of the owners' family and we cannot find any record of who she might be.